NLP

A Psychologist's Guide To Mastering Influence And Human Behaviour Through The Art Of Personal Mind Control In Order To Maximise Your Potential For Excellence

Armin Ritter

TABLE OF CONTENT

What Is Nlp?..1

The Art Of Influencing Others Via Language...10

How To Make Your Morning Routine More Productive, Positive, And Confident In Your Own Ability To Succeed!..23

When To Make New Goals, What Kinds Of Rewards To Give Yourself, And How To Keep Your Motivation At An All-Time High! 26

A Concise Explanation On Why You Ought To Create A Budget..37

Identify Points Of Similarity 43

Secret Manipulation Of Events 55

The Four Fundamental Ideas Of Nlp 64

Mantras Are Both Powerful Tools And Powerful Tools In Their Own Right..79

During A Session Of Self-Hypnosis, There Are Several Things That Should Be Avoided At All Costs..103

Mastery Of The Art Of Persuasion......................113

Why Should You Get Training In Hypnotic Persuasion Skills?..120

Several Factors That Should Be Kept In Mind 146

How Can I Reprogram My Mind To Get Rid Of Stress, Anxiety, Fear, And Depression? What Are The Steps? 160

What Is Nlp?

Neuro Linguistic Programming is what the abbreviation NLP refers to. It is the study of people's reactions to a certain stimulus. If you take each of the three terms and split them down into their respective components, the word "neuro" refers to the part of our nervous system that controls how the body works. It is accountable for all that we perceive, including what we see, feel, taste, touch, and hear. The term "linguistic" refers to the language that we use to communicate with other people as well as to organise our thoughts and actions. When we talk about language, we also include the non-verbal sort of communication that goes on between people, which is known as body language. The word "programming" refers to the way in which our minds (neuro) and the language we use (linguistic) interact with one another to define our behaviours.

NLP is useful for studying how individuals behave, how they think, how they take in information and how they respond to what they have taken in. NLP consists of a number of straightforward and useful methods, all of which are geared particularly at assisting you in making positive changes in your life. Through the use of your one-of-a-kind sensory experiences, linguistic abilities, and talents in the art of persuasion, it assists in bringing about a shift in your thoughts and actions, which finally results in a change in your behaviour.

NLP techniques are often employed in the area of psychology to assist therapists in achieving immediate and long term changes in their patients. NLP is a technique for altering the behaviour of the brain via the use of language and other types of communication; as such, these approaches fall under the category of a technique. But as more time has gone, individuals from a variety of different disciplines, such as teaching, training, business, law, and sales, have also begun employing it for the purposes of personal development, improvement of performance, and the accomplishment of their objectives. Techniques from the field of neurolinguistic programming (NLP) are increasingly appearing in books on topics such as corporate communication and self-help.

Imagine gaining access to the potent Mind Changing Tools that have been designed specifically for the purpose of enhancing and addressing any and all aspects of your life.

NLP is very helpful for many different applications, including the following:

1. Altering the way you think about things

2. Assist in the process of finding answers to your questions

3. If you want to be successful, you need to change your behaviours and mental patterns.

4. Making your emotions work for you; 5. Improving yourself and maximising your performance; 6. Taking command of your thoughts and actions

7. Assists you in gaining and maintaining the drive necessary to accomplish your objectives in a timely manner

8. In addition to this, it enables you to better manage stress and concentrate on the things you want to do.

A Journey Inside of Your Thoughts

It is really crucial that you comprehend your state of mind before we go further with this. Have you ever given any attention to the way in which your mind truly functions? Where does the process of thinking begin, and where does it end?

Your mind is an extremely strong weapon that, when put to work properly, can do miracles for you. If you put it to work right, it can do marvels for you.

It is my hope that at the end of this chapter, you will have a better comprehension of the phrases "conscious mind" and "subconscious mind." These are two terms that are used very often by everyone, yet nobody ever truly understands what anybody means by them. First things first, let's have a good grasp on the difference between the conscious mind and the subconscious mind.

In most people, the mind may be broken down into three distinct layers: the conscious mind, the subconscious mind, and the unconscious mind. For the time being, we are only going to be concerned with the conscious and the subconscious mind. Your conscious mind is also referred to as the rational level, whereas the level of your subconscious mind that controls your behaviour is known as the illogical level. Both of these facets of your mind operate in a distinctive manner, and it is critical to comprehend how each one does its job.

The part of your thinking known as your conscious mind is the part of your mind in which you exercise total command over your ideas. You are well aware of the fact that your thoughts might be "good," "bad," "happy," "sad," and so on. You may choose to actively invite either good or bad ideas into your head. Either way, you will experience both. When you think about such things with full awareness, you are inadvertently leaving an impact on your subconscious mind, which is the part of your mind that is often responsible for doing the job behind the scenes. Whatever you think works its way down into your subconscious mind, which then programming it and turns it into your normal way of thinking. This pattern of thought causes you to behave in the manner that you have previously predetermined in your subconscious mind. Your mind's subconscious would never challenge your conscious judgement about what's morally acceptable and what should be avoided. The information that is being provided into the system will simply be stored in it, and it will respond to your activities in the manner specified by that information.

Permit me to illustrate this to you using a straightforward example taken from your normal day-to-day activities. It is customary to wash one's hands immediately upon completion of one's meal. You don't give your mind a direct order to go wash your hands; it just happens. Is it not so?

Now, I want you to go back to the first time someone requested you to wash your hands after you had eaten a meal. Visualise that moment in your mind as if it were yesterday. After that, you had begun to give your mind the instruction to wash your hands after each meal intentionally. Your subconscious mind was impacted by that idea of yours, and it was subsequently logged there. As a result of repeatedly engaging in the same behaviour, it eventually solidified itself as a habit, and you now routinely wash your hands after each meal. Your formerly conscious activity has thus morphed into an action that you now do automatically in your mind. This illustrates the fundamental difference in operation between your conscious mind and your subconscious mind.

Your conscious mind and your subconscious mind are both very essential to comprehend, but there is one more thing that you really must know about both. Words like "no," "don't," "not," and "never" are foreign concepts to the part of our brains that processes memories and emotions. Because our subconscious mind does not comprehend and record these phrases, you will need to learn to rephrase them into a different form so that your subconscious mind will have a picture that corresponds to what you truly want it to have.

Permit me to give you an example of this, and I will show you what I mean when I say that our subconscious mind does not grasp those phrases. Follow my instructions to the letter down here.

Warning: You are not allowed to think about a black cat.

What was the first thing that sprung into your head?

A mysterious feline! Is it not so?

Did it finally click for you that your subconscious mind is incapable of comprehending the word 'not'? As a result, we need to think very critically about the kinds of things we let to into our unconscious mind.

The Art Of Influencing Others Via Language

Both the art of persuasion and the art of influence go hand in hand. Both are regarded as forms of art rather than sciences, despite the fact that their significance may be seen in a variety of living domains. When it comes to having influence on another person, it is important to have the ability to persuade that person to change his mind, mould his view, or be prompted to make choices. Because our teams are becoming more flat, matrixed, and flatter, the concept of "power" is no longer entirely dependent on one's position in the hierarchy. Now, the one who has greater authority is the one who can influence more people.

You need to be able to combine flair with substance if you want to be a successful influencer in the world. Establishing a strong foundation of trustworthiness is of utmost importance, therefore make sure you do that. If any of these conditions are met, your most effective method of attack will be to use persuasive language.

Techniques of persuasion each have their own amount of effectiveness. Whether you are a novice, an intermediate user, or an experienced user of tactics of persuasion, you should be able to determine when to deploy these strategies to ensure that they have the most possible impact on the target audience.

There are twenty different methods of persuasion and influence that you might try.

Techniques of Basic Influence and Argumentation

1. By Common Experience

People who are still in the beginning stages of developing their ability to influence others often use this particular kind of persuasion since it has a high rate of success. When using this strategy, you make an effort to establish a connection between the specific service, product, or concept in question and another aspect that your target audience already enjoys. Association is a strong method, even if it does not guarantee that you will be able to accomplish the aforementioned goals in a categorical manner.

Take Coca-Cola as an example; for many years, one of the most successful marketing strategies has been to employ emotional transfer to link the idea of "family" with the company's product and get consumers to feel a connection to it. Additionally, the brand 'Nike' has been linked to the word 'winning' in recent years.

Bandwagon, Number Two

The bandwagon method is yet another approach to persuasion that is appropriate for beginners to make use of. To put it simply, what you want to do is to convince other people see that 'everyone else is already doing it and so should you'. The vast majority of individuals like to feel as if they belong somewhere, and they do not wish to lag behind others. As a result, the primary objective of this strategy is to establish whether or not the prospective customer is prepared to join you on the bandwagon.

3. Referring to Testimonials

Okay, so this is most likely one of the most often used approaches, but in spite of the fact that it has been around for many years, it continues to be quite effective. This is due to the fact that people in general pay a heightened level of attention to celebrities. Following a celebrity or being a fan is one of the guilty pleasures that everyone may have, regardless of whether or not we confess it to ourselves. It is much simpler to persuade consumers to test a product when a well-known celebrity, athlete, or model endorses the brand in question.

4. By Making Use of Humour

The reason why many of the commercials stick in our memories is because of the humorous elements that were included in them. When we are in the same room with them, we can't help but smile and chuckle. As a result, it is a very effective method of persuasion. It is much simpler to persuade individuals to move in a certain direction when you link your wares or services to something that improves their well-being. This holds true when it comes to interpersonal connections as well. When you can make someone laugh in a way that demonstrates both your intelligence and your sense of humour, it is much simpler to maintain that person's like of you over time.

5. Through Constant Practise

They claim that practising something several times is the best way to remember it. You need to be able to quietly and creatively repeat your message if you want to be able to influence and convince other people. Have you ever discovered that a commercial jingle was stuck in your mind and you couldn't stop humming or singing it? You may not like the product itself, but due to the fact that you see the advertisement almost every day on the Internet, on television, or even in print advertisements, something about it has stuck with you.When it sinks in, influencing a person is a lot easier since there is a lot less resistance.

#6. As Suggested By Professionals

Additionally, this may be considered a testimonial. It is not uncommon for folks to investigate the rationale behind a certain item as well as the claims made by experts about it. If you are an expert in a certain field, it will be much simpler to locate a testimony from another expert in that field. For instance, if the majority of your potential consumers are parents or mothers, then the individual serving in the expert role should also be a mother who is well-versed in the relevant subject matter.

#7: By Taking a Bribe

Absolutely, none of us can resist a good freebie; don't we? You may use this strategy as well if you so want. If you want to have greater influence on people, offer them more than they anticipate, such as a discount, a promotion, holidays, and so on. To have influence over people also requires having the ability to provide them with a fair return on their investments, excellent value for the money they spend, and so on. As you improve your abilities, you will eventually be in a position to exert greater influence utilising the strategies that are detailed in the following paragraphs.

Techniques of Persuasion at an Intermediate Level

8. By Exemplifying a Charismatic Attitude

I have to confess that I am very much responsible for doing this. When the product endorser is someone who interests me in their own right, I'm more likely to go ahead and make the purchase. For instance, you may anticipate that people will pay greater attention to what you have to say if you show yourself as being daring, confident, powerful, and stylish.

#9. By Introducing Unconventional Concepts

People like learning about new stuff. It should come as no surprise that a lot of people put a lot of confidence in new technical developments. One strategy for influencing people's opinions is to provide them with information that is novel to them. Please take note that a variety of emotional triggers were explored in the chapter before this one. They will feel a feeling of accomplishment from the fact that they were among the first to get something unique if you provide it to them.

10th Place: Making Use of Rhetorical Questions

Asking questions of individuals is one of the most efficient strategies for eliciting responses from other people. Questions such as "Do you want to become a millionaire before you hit 30?", "Do you want to live debt-free?", and "Do you want to be as stunning as Monica Bellucci?" are all put up to generate alignment and to establish rapport before the sales pitch takes over. These are the kinds of questions that, in most cases, will attract the interest of your prospect, encouraging them to remain for a longer period of time and listen to the sales presentation.

11. In Memory of Nostalgia

This approach is the polar opposite of procedure number 9. In this strategy, you attempt to exert influence over other individuals by arousing their nostalgia for the "good old days." There are some individuals who, in response to the quick pace of change, find that they are becoming exhausted by it and long for the days when life was far less complicated. An excellent illustration of this would be the resurgence of the Nokia 3310 in this age of technologically powerful smartphones or the easy-to-prepare meals that evokes fond childhood memories.

#12: By Providing Convenient and Straightforward Answers

Because of the complexity of the environment in which we live, individuals are always looking for ways to simplify problems. If you want to sway someone's opinion or the opinion of a target audience, make their life easier by suggesting a straightforward answer to any issue. For example, advertisers enjoy the idea of a 'one-stop-shop' for any given service since it allows customers to fulfil a variety of requirements in a single location, which is convenient for the customers.

#13, By Demonstrating a Dangerous Decline

This is somewhat analogous to using 'fear' as a weapon for the purpose of exerting influence. You may have more influence on people if, rather than anticipating favourable outcomes, you show them the impending hazards that might occur if they do not act and make a choice as soon as possible. For instance, in order to influence and convince people to invest, you may highlight the probable situations when the recession starts up in order to influence and encourage people to invest. This strategy allows for the use of anything that might paint a picture for the individual of what can occur as a result of their failure to take action.

#14, by Offering Support from the Scientific Community

You will have the opportunity to give facts in this approach, which will ultimately lead someone to make a choice immediately after hearing them. Many people have the habit of thinking of themselves as "people of Science," which refers to those who are interested in learning the scientific theory behind a product before purchasing it. For example, if you are attempting to sell a skin care product that contains collagen, you need to describe the function that collagen plays in the biological constitution of the skin and what it accomplishes in order to successfully sell the product. It's possible that displaying advertising with attractive women utilising the product won't be enough.

You are going to discover the strategies that advanced level influencers employ in the next things that are going to be displayed to you, so pay attention to what is being presented. Take into account that you are not compelled to look at this list straight immediately. You may test out any of the options on the list that came before this one to see which one complements your sense of style the most.

How To Make Your Morning Routine More Productive, Positive, And Confident In Your Own Ability To Succeed!

When you first open your eyes in the morning, there are a few things you can do to set the tone for a more upbeat and optimistic day. This will assist you throughout the day to boost your productivity and improve your self-confidence, allowing you to continue making progress towards achieving your objective and getting closer to achieving it.

Cheer up! Smile as soon as you open your eyes because you have been given another chance to make the most of life and another day to count your blessings. Appreciate the fact that you are still alive and find joy in the fact that you still have this opportunity.

Stretch your muscles out. Relax your muscles and your body. Check that you are really awake and able to take on the challenges of the new day. The increased blood flow that results with stretching is beneficial.

Just be sure you keep breathing normally. Doing workouts that require slow and deep breathing should be a deliberate effort on your part. This helps to oxygenate all of your cells to their maximum capacity. This routine will keep you attentive and energised throughout the day.

Take in some water. Consuming water will assist your body with the shift. You just finished the "fasting" phase, therefore it's important that you rehydrate now.

Get off the bed and get some fresh air. Get up and start moving! Don't simply lie there doing nothing. Seize the opportunity!

Maintain a connection with your own feelings. Put your attention on the positive. Keep your attention on the things that interest you. Put your attention on the affection you have for your family.

Keep your attention fixed on your long-term vision, purpose, and goals. Utilise methods such as meditation and visualisation to help you maintain your concentration on the goals you have set for yourself about what you want to accomplish in your life. Keep in mind that your energy will go in the same direction as your concentrate.

When To Make New Goals, What Kinds Of Rewards To Give Yourself, And How To Keep Your Motivation At An All-Time High!

When you have a clear vision of where you want to go, it doesn't matter how long or winding the path to get there is; what matters is that you stay focused on getting there.

So, after you've accomplished what you set out to achieve, what comes next?

Put in another attempt! It is a process that never comes to a conclusion. You don't give up simply because you've accomplished one of your goals; you keep going. There are still a great many things that are within your reach to achieve.

But do not rush into working on another objective just now; give it some more time. You are deserving of a reward, therefore give it to yourself. You don't need to come up with something too creative. Everyone should be commended for a job well done, and it is clear that you have gone above and beyond the call of duty.

Even if the fact that you finally have the home of your dreams is a reward in and of itself, you should still find a way to encourage yourself in some way. This will help you remain motivated and excited for the next adventure you take.

There are many different methods that you may reward not just yourself but also your family. You may begin by treating yourself to a complete body massage. Your physical self deserves some TLC since it has gone through so much effort on your behalf to make it possible for you to purchase the home of your dreams. Do something nice for yourself, like getting a new outfit or a new pair of shoes. You should celebrate your achievement by going out with your close friends. Simple activities such as these are what keep your energy levels up.

Or, you could be thinking that it would be fun to take the entire family away for the weekend. If you want something less complicated, you might simply treat everyone to a straightforward lunch or dinner in your house, where all of your other family will be able to join in on the festivities.

Are you prepared to establish a new objective for yourself?

When you reflect on your trip, you could recognise the errors that you made and the difficulties that you faced that came dangerously close to preventing you from achieving your objective; but, despite all of these obstacles, you were able to overcome them and you were ultimately successful. You might look at your mistakes as opportunities for learning, so that the next time you come into similar situations, you'll be more prepared and know exactly what to do.

When you are still elated after a recent victory, it is simple to establish another objective for yourself, and doing so may serve as a powerful motivator. When you succeed in accomplishing your objective, your level of self-confidence will get a significant increase.

After taking a day break from activities related to your goal, you may start the process of creating a new goal to put your attention on. It is not necessary for one's aspirations to be as momentous as the acquisition of a home or vehicle. It is possible that you may start concentrating on providing for the further education of your children. Because you have just completed a previous objective, you now have a better understanding of how to handle monetary concerns, making it simpler for you to complete the following objective.

Just have a good attitude and keep pushing yourself forward. Your brand-new house is more than enough reason to get moving. It is already a tremendous complement to your talents and abilities, as well as to what you are capable of doing with pure dedication and by working hard. Every time you think about what you had to go through to get it, it is a huge tribute to your skills and abilities.

Do not accept anything less than what you really want; instead, formulate specific objectives, keep your attention on those objectives, and put in a lot of effort.

Alter Your Routines

Consider the most recent time you went away on a vacation. There is no need that the trip be an extended one either. Simply taking a few days off to get away from it all, seeing new places, people, and cuisine, engaging in entertaining activities while you're gone, and letting go of your worries can provide you with a surge of vitality.

You may not even be aware of the shift in perspective until it has already occurred. You are going to have a new perspective on yourself as well as others.

This is the primary reason why individuals feel compelled to alter their plans for where they would spend their vacation. This strategy is doomed to failure due to the fact that we are creatures of habit, and the very nature of our daily lives ensures that we will revert to our previous ways of thinking.

Your will to life will dwindle if you allow yourself to get mired in routines. Breaking the monotony of your daily activities may be accomplished with as little as a modicum of effort on your part.

A Brand New Ten Percent

Every person should have a routine that helps their life run smoothly and allows them to get things done in the most time-efficient manner possible.

Those routines that never come to an end and never get shaken up are not helpful. You need to provide yourself with the "ten percent new" in order to strike a balance here. This will provide you with the task of trying something new every day for the next two weeks.

Listed below are some easy things that you might try:

Introduce yourself to new individuals.

Try out some new meals.

Wear a new outfit.

Alter up your shopping routine by going somewhere different.

Take a break from cooking during the middle of the week and dine out.

Switch up the sequence in which you complete the tasks.

Take a new route on the way to work today.

Because you may add your own thoughts and suggestions to this list, it might go on forever.

Basically, all you need to do is start making some moderate adjustments, and then maintain those modifications for a full fortnight. Put yourself in their position and experience the change.

You could maintain a diary to keep note of what you do and what occurs, but this would only be useful for those who are sceptical or who like keeping diaries. If you already maintain one, by all means track this, but if you don't, then there's no need for you to start keeping one simply so you can keep track of what you are doing.

Really Only Ten Percent?

There are a lot of folks for whom making a lot of changes won't work out well. It will only serve to stir up opposition. It won't be effective, and all it will do is cause disruption. It is challenging to maintain the forward momentum.

You are need to make just minor adjustments. Because of this, a difference of ten percent is preferable than a difference of ninety percent. This provides an introduction to making modest modifications, which, by themselves, are sufficient to break one out of everyday ruts. Consider the magnitude of the shift that may occur over the course of a year if you make adjustments of around 10 percent every day.

Why are It's Important to Focus, Have Energy, and Time?

Your capacity for concentration, energy, and time is not infinite. Each of them is going to run out at some time. In order to get the most out of these resources, we have to make smart use of them. For this reason, it is vital to be organised and to prepare ahead.

Just Before You Get Started

If you don't start by having clarity in these four areas, your strategy is doomed to fail before it ever gets off the ground.

In what direction do you anticipate your life heading in the years to come?

Set yourself some manageable milestones along the road so you can track your progress.

The primary areas of emphasis that will eventually lead to the things that you have to concentrate on right now.

The most important aspects to work on are determining what qualities and abilities are necessary to achieve your ultimate objectives.

A Concise Explanation On Why You Ought To Create A Budget

Having a comprehensive strategy for your budget will allow you to take a logical and organised approach to the management of your finances. Consider a budget plan to be a useful financial tool that you may use to keep track of how much money you spend and how much you put away at the conclusion of a certain time period. It is advised that you create a budget plan either weekly or monthly (to match with a monthly paycheck), since this is the most common scenario. The easiest approach for you to understand how your financial behaviour is based on a framework that is both structured and purposeful is to look at it in this manner.

To be fair, creating a budget is neither the most interesting nor the most alluring activity in the whole world. People are quite unlikely to boast about the fact that they are successfully adhering to a stringent financial plan. There is, however, no ignoring the fact that one of the most crucial tools that you can employ to keep your financial situation in order is a well-thought-out budget plan. This is particularly important to keep in mind when you are responsible for managing the budget of a home that includes numerous persons whose levels of income and requirements might vary greatly from one another.

When it comes down to it, budgeting is really all about maintaining a sense of equilibrium. You should be aware at this point that you do not have a limitless quantity of money available to you. You have no doubt already acquired the knowledge necessary to find other sources of revenue. On the other hand, you should never expect to have a limitless supply of resources. In light of this, you need to keep a close eye on the way in which you are spending the money that you earn. It is important to keep in mind that if you spend money on one thing, it will reduce the amount of money you have available to spend on anything other. If you want to put a bit more money towards your monthly groceries, for instance, that can mean you have to reduce the amount of money you spend dining out with your family at restaurants. Your ability to put money down for your children's college education can be hindered if you have a propensity for going on shopping binges and spending more than you intended to.

Consequently, a budget will assist you in determining how to reach that ideal financial balance that will place you in the greatest position to thrive financially and discover the fulfilment that comes along with it. Obviously, you shouldn't simply save money for the sake of saving money all the time, but at the same time, you shouldn't be careless with your money either. You have to find that sweet spot when everything is just right. This is what it means to have a meaningful attitude to how you earn and spend your money, so keep this in mind.

How to Make a Plan for Your Budget

Creating a strategy for one's budget may be done using any number of different approaches. It is quite similar to adopting a diet as a technique for the purpose of losing weight. People seek to maintain a healthy weight in a variety of ways, including adhering to one of the many available diet programmes. Some individuals have a stronger preference for low-carb diets, while others have a natural tendency to respond better to a more well-rounded approach to dieting. It's the same thing with making plans for your budget. As you continue your investigation, you will discover that there are many distinct methods of financial planning and savings. That is a really positive development. This way, if a certain approach to budgeting does not work for you, you have access to a variety of different strategies that could.

Having saying that, when it comes to designing your personal budget plan, there are a few guiding concepts that you want to make sure stay in the back of your mind. Do not be concerned if you would want to create one from scratch but are unclear how to go about doing so if this is what you intend to do. This part of the chapter will walk you through, step by step, the process of creating a personal budget plan that works for you and your unique circumstances. You won't have to approach it in the dark if you do it this way. When one does not know where to begin with their financial responsibilities, it may be challenging to navigate their way through those responsibilities. However, if you have the appropriate guiding principles in place, you will discover that it is more simpler than you first anticipated.

Identify Points Of Similarity

People are drawn to those with whom they share characteristics and interests. You might give yourself the same concept by creating the illusion that you and someone else have a lot of things in common. That allows you to create trust and chemistry between the two of you.

Even if they aren't familiar with you yet, the individual will develop a stronger like for you as a result of this.

When people feel this way towards you, it greatly increases the likelihood that they will agree with what you say and desire to follow your advice. This is due to the fact that they get the impression that you know them and that they can put their faith in you to make suggestions for them that would eventually work out in their favour or profit.

It was an easy decision for me to make given how much I like unwinding after a long day at work by watching television as I eat supper. I am aware that you like football as much as I do, and you owe it to yourself to check out how the game seems on a TV equipped with such a high resolution! It's almost as if you're there, seeing everything unfold in real time!

In this particular instance, we will make the assumption that you have already identified some commonalities and discovered that your customer has an interest in football and values having the very best available to them. You will also have the chance to overcome any financial resistance that they may have against the goods. As can be seen, having something in common with the person you are influencing provides you "pull" with them.

Finding points of resemblance is a simple process. It results from first connecting with what another person is saying and then offering facts that that person would find relevant.

For instance, if they mention that they prefer the colour red, you should also like it. Then, at a later time, you might add something along the lines of, "That is my favourite ____, especially because it comes in the colour red!" You have not mentioned very clearly that it is available to them in red at this point.

Instead, you've said how much you like the colour red and how it gets your blood pumping. They are more likely to feel as if they are like you since they would also be the kind to become thrilled about this knowledge because you already know that they enjoy the colour red and you already know that they like it.

You can do this with almost anything you want to. For instance, if you are out on a date with someone, you may show that you two have a lot in common by discussing how you feel about your work, your ambitions, and your life in general. You and your date may find common ground by first listening to the memories that each of you has to offer with the other and then talking about your own experiences that are comparable.

In the end, you are able to create an environment in which people have the impression that they understand you. You are familiar with them, despite the fact that the two of you may know very little about one another.

Establishing similarities via body language is another viable option. Although this strategy is more of a kind of persuasion, it is nevertheless very important in the process of manipulation. This is accomplished by master manipulators using a strategy that is referred to as "pacing." That implies that they effectively mimic a person's body language and utilise their clues, including both verbal and non-verbal cues, to create the impression that they are the same person.

Because you act in a manner that is comparable to that of your subject, they receive the impression that you are similar to them on a fundamentally psychological level. They may not realise it consciously, but their subconscious mind will realise that you are imitating them, and it will interpret this as an indication that you and your topic have a lot of similarities. Although they may not recognise it consciously, their subconscious mind will realise that you are copying them.

You should never be too blatant while doing this, but mirroring them to some degree is a fantastic way to build your morale with them and enhance the pull you have when getting them to do what you want them to do. In other words, it is a terrific approach to get them to do what you want them to do.

1The deceitful manipulator will tell you that you are to blame for any and all difficulties that arise in any circumstance. When someone is manipulating you, the person doing the manipulating will never confess that they have ever done anything wrong. According to them, this is not even somewhat possible. To them, the only thing that can be true is that you did something wrong, and it is hard to convince them that they had any involvement in it since the only other explanation that makes sense to them is that you did something wrong. This problem arises because people have an extremely egocentric perspective on the world. When someone has these thoughts, they will tell you things like, "If you were on my side, you wouldn't do that." This is a clear indication that they have these beliefs. It goes on like this: "If I matter to you, you have no choice but to believe this," and so on. As a manipulator of psychology yourself, you should be able to see that this is an example of framing. Unfortunately, they are utilising framing in an abusive manner, which means that they are trying to exonerate themselves of any responsibility for the problem while shifting all of the blame onto someone else. It makes no difference what the actual truth is, nor does it matter how drastically the picture painted by the artist does not correspond to the actual world that can be seen by everybody. They will not accept the truth if it makes them appear worse than they already do. Not only is this an excellent method for determining whether or not you are being manipulated, but it is also an excellent illustration of how not to utilise framing. Because, for one thing, it is abusive to never accept any framing that makes you appear terrible, but also because it is plain ineffective NLP, you should never do this. This method of psychological manipulation is ineffective. Just because you continue to claim that something is real does not mean that others will accept blatant falsehoods for a very long time. They will believe it for a little period of time, but after that, they will get weary of you and stop believing what you say. In the course of your manipulation of psychology, you shouldn't make this error.

2) The nefarious manipulator will never acknowledge the validity of any legitimate challenge to their framework. Because if you want people to embrace your vision of the truth on an issue, you can't simply double down on your frame without altering it, this is yet another example of how a malevolent manipulator is also not a good one. If you want people to believe your vision of the truth on a matter, you can't just double down on your frame. A manipulator with harmful intentions will not modify their framing. They are unyielding in their refusal to adjust to the new information provided by the subject, which threatens the integrity of the existing framework. If you have the audacity to dispute their flawed framework, they will tell you that "You're not seeing things straight,"

which means that your perspective is skewed. "How is it that you can be so wrong?" Also, keep in mind how rude the malevolent manipulator may be at times. This in no way helps the process of NLP to be more successful. If you want to be able to influence the subject's thinking or manipulate them, they do not necessarily need to like you totally, but they do need to appreciate who you are as a person. When you treat other people as if they don't matter, it doesn't take long for them to lose respect for you, and once that occurs, you can forget about using psychology or other forms of psychological manipulation on them.

3) The confidence that an NLP practitioner has to have in order to influence others is not the same as the confidence that a malevolent manipulator has. They have such enormous egos that it really works against them when it comes to achieving good long-term results with NLP. At this time, their self-assurance has reached an inhuman level. You should take NLP

practitioners like this as an example of what not to do as a lesson, because this sort of behaviour is not successful, and more importantly, it is not sustainable. You should take this as a lesson in what not to do. There are perhaps some individuals in the world who can be captivated by one's unbridled assurance, but it's unlikely that there are very many of them, and even if there are, they won't be for very long. To start, there is no need that you centre your mind control or manipulations on yourself. In the vast majority of instances, in point of fact, you want to disassociate yourself from the actual content that you alter in their head so that it may exist independently from you. You may want to make them like you subconsciously at first, but because you don't want them to link you with the information that was altered in their mind, you also don't want them to perceive you as being related to what you mind control or manipulate. Sure, at first, you could want to make them like you unintentionally. They will assume that the only thing that occurred was that they altered their thoughts or behaviour on their own as a result of this. Because the majority of people wish to use psychological manipulation for good, it is likely that the majority of the time, engaging in these behaviours and believing these things will be beneficial for you. However, this does not imply that you should try to convince the subject to perceive things in this light since doing so is counterproductive to NLP. When they do it just for themselves and not for the benefit of others, those who engage in manipulative behaviour are losing out on the full potential of NLP.

Secret Manipulation Of Events

The technique of covert manipulation is often cited as one of the most risky approaches used in dark psychology. It entails methodically diminishing one person's authority in such a covert and deniable manner that the subject normally is unaware that it has occurred to them at any point in time. They may have a sudden realisation that they do not know how they have arrived to a certain place in their life, and they may feel as if they have no idea where they are or what they should do. They may feel lost and bewildered, but they may not know what to do. Although this is often seen as being somewhat immoral, it is yet essential to have this understanding.

The Meaning of the Term "Covert Manipulation"

When you engage in covert manipulation, what you're really doing is trying to figure out what makes the other person tick so that you can effectively deconstruct them as a person and reassemble them into something entirely new. It often entails playing with the other person's vulnerabilities in such a covert and secretive manner that the other person is never aware that anything is occurring. These deeds are carried out in a manner that enables the manipulator to maintain control over the circumstance while also making it possible for them to conceal their connection to the occurrence. This is done slowly at first, and then gradually increased in speed until the task at hand is finished.

In order to comprehend covert manipulation, one must first comprehend what the terms signify in and of themselves. The word "covert" alludes to the discrete and stealthy aspect of the action, which takes place fully in the background. The manipulator's goal is to maintain their covert role as the unseen puppeteer, manipulating all of the strings while seeming as innocent as possible to everyone around them. This is accomplished by disguising oneself behind the concept of plausible deniability, which means that the person in question is able to assert that they were not responsible for the act in question while yet making it seem logical and believable that they were not. Second, you need to have an understanding of what it means to manipulate someone, which is the act of convincing someone to engage in behaviour that is not in their best interest and is not in accordance with their own free will.

When you choose to influence someone covertly, you are essentially taking control of their mind; you are destroying everything they believed they knew and thought while doing it behind their back in a manner that leaves you unscathed. In other words, you are hijacking their mind. By persuading someone to comply with whatever it is you want, you are reducing them to nothing more than a puppet with no free will and turning them into a mere extension of yourself. You are, in effect, brainwashing someone else so that they would accept your directions and perform what you consider to be advantageous for yourself and no one else.

When you are seeking to surreptitiously influence someone else into compliance, it is important to keep in mind that you are, in essence, exploiting them in that endeavour. You are robbing them of their free will and their own individuality, and in its place you are creating someone who will comply. Because doing so fundamentally dehumanises another person, you should never do so to someone you care about or hold in high regard.

Processes Involved in Covert Manipulation

The idea behind covert manipulation is relatively straightforward, despite the sneaky nature of the practise: It is accomplished in three stages. If you want to influence another person, you need to follow these three stages in order to increase the likelihood that your efforts will be successful and to your advantage. The following describes each of these three stages:

After following the procedures, you will be left with a person who is so uncertain and concerned about his or her own ability to think and make judgements that he or she would happily defer to you out of ease. The individual will comply with whatever it is that you ask of them since it is simpler for them to do so than it is for them to come to their own conclusions on their own. The puppet that the manipulator has been striving to construct is all that is left behind once all is said and done. At this stage, the manipulator is in a position to focus on fine-tuning the activities of the target, making certain that inappropriate behaviour or failing to carry out what is desired would result in repercussions.

Infiltration of the Circle Surrounding the Target

Learning is the first stage in the process of covert manipulation. You need to gather as much information is can about the target before you can start building an arsenal of weapons that will finally enable you to exert complete control over the other person. Begin by making an effort to enter the person's inner circle of friends and associates. If you want to be in a position to exert influence on the target, you have to be able to win that person's friendship.

This may be accomplished by seeming to be interested in the topic, even when, deep down, you really are. You are more interested in gaining knowledge that will benefit you in the future as opposed to gaining knowledge about what makes the other person tick for the sole purpose of gaining knowledge about that other person. You are faking a connection with the other person by trying to figure out what their passions are and what it is about them that allows them to operate as a human while you are learning about those things. You want the other person to like you, and perhaps maybe love you, yet at the same time you want to maintain control of the current situation.

As soon as you have established the level of trust required to be let into the inner circle of your target, you will begin receiving all of the information that you need and require. This is when you will begin learning more about the other person, and the more intimate the facts, the greater the likelihood that you will be able to utilise the details in the future as weapons.

Collect All of Your Weapons

You will start to acquire the important information after your connection with the individual, or more specifically the other person's attachment and confidence in you, has developed further. You will most likely discover all there is to know about the family life of the other person, in addition to their sensitivities, beliefs, and other profound, personal ideas that may come in handy in the future.

You are currently gathering information about the individual's shortcomings at this stage. You want to find out where all of the chips in his or her metaphorical armour are located, as well as precisely grasp what you will need to do in order to transform a chip into a crack, as well as what you will need to do in order to make a crack in the armour cause the armour as a whole to shatter.

You are going to want to engage in additional conversation with the target during this. You should practise reading his or her unique body language so that you can tell as much as possible about the person's motivations and activities with as little effort as feasible. When you are at this stage, you will start to grasp the other person's worries, as well as their ideas, goals, and ambitions for the future, as well as anything else that may be presented to you at this time. At this stage, the other person will feel fairly secure in the connection, particularly if you have been pretending to be interested in the relationship or potentially even love bombing to drive it along. At this time, the relationship will have progressed quite a bit. This is exactly what you want to happen; you want that sense of security, that sense of connection, to grow because it is this attachment that will serve as your anchor to keeping the other person around, despite the fact that they may manipulate and abuse you. Even if the other person discovers the abusive behaviour, it will be more difficult for them to break free of it if they are strongly linked to the person who is abusing them.

The Four Fundamental Ideas OfNlp

According to Thomas H. Huxley, "the greatest achievement in life is not knowledge, but action." [Citation needed]

To learn the many approaches that NLP has to offer, it is essential to first grasp these four basic concepts.

Each of these guiding principles is relevant to both your personal life and the way you interact with other people. They place an emphasis on how you communicate, how you plan your objectives, what you want to accomplish in life, what qualities you possess, and how you can accept and respect the differences in others.

You will be able to acquire interested in NLP and these areas of study, and you will be able to determine which ones you want to spend more time on. This is true regardless of the line of work that you already have.

Reporting, meaning, outcomes, and flexibility in behaviour are the four pillars around which NLP is founded.

1. Give a report

Establishing rapport (also known as harmony) is critical for successful communication. It is accomplished via individuals treating one another with respect, and the majority of the time it is achieved on an instinctive level. It involves focus and concentration since you must pay attention to the circumstance at hand rather than just thinking about anything else in your head instead of being present in the moment.

It demands you to display real attention, observe the other person's response to what you are saying, and recognise the essential words or phrases that are being used in the conversation. El Rapporto isn't only tied to your words, but also to your body language and language that you generally don't even realise you're using.

The manner in which you communicate will change depending on the context as well as the mode of contact (whether it be by phone, email, or in person).

It is vital to be aware of how people communicate and how to employ gestures, body postures, tone of voice, words, and other forms of expression in order to construct this harmony.

Confluence and Reflections both come to mind.

The confluence and reflection procedures were developed by Milton Erickson in the early 1970s as part of his work on therapeutic hypnotherapy. These techniques are now used as part of the Report building process. since of this, body language is important since you are attempting to imitate the body language of the person you are having a conversation with. This becomes abundantly evident when one observes young couples, each of them instinctively copies the bodily movements of the other (touching their hair in the same manner, sitting or stopping in the same manner, etc.). If you watch the patrons of restaurants carefully, you'll be able to notice how they are mirrored in the atmosphere.

Confluence and reflection take place in a manner that is usually unnoticed and unobtrusive in everyday dialogue. Mimicking someone else's body posture, employing gestures that are similar to theirs, and speaking in the same tone and cadence may be an effective technique to build rapport with another person.

The activity of reporting

Convergence and reflection are two strong forces; put them to the test by participating in this activity with your peers.

Determine who in a group of three persons will be person A, person B, and person C.

vs.

Person A will discuss for one minute about an experience (like a party) that they had that they enjoyed very much.

a pastime activity, etc. Person B will pay attention, and at first, they will attempt to mimic the motions and postures of person A. Person A will continue to talk while person B will then perform the reverse of what person A is doing (creating gestures that no longer correlate with person A). In the end, person B will do the exact identical motions and postures that person A did once again.

Person C is observing the happenings in the situation.

This exercise calls for imitation, followed by anti-reflection, and then another round of reflection. After completing the activity, you should exchange roles so that everyone gets to experience everything. Permit person C to share their thoughts on what they saw. When Person A's body language is no longer being imitated by Person B, it is often extremely difficult for Person A to continue the conversation.

When the choice is made to change, the process of doing so is simple. This may be accomplished with a sign, a phrase, or an act. If there is a need for change, then it is necessary to implement the change.

I decided to drive my automobile to the seaside in order to get away from the familiar sights that were around me. What I really wanted was a view of the ocean, but I ended up booking a room at a less expensive hotel with a view of the surrounding landscape instead. This was the cost of reserving one of the few rooms that were still available. I gazed about at the vegetation of the terrain, and my attention was drawn to a lone tree that was growing very slowly atop a hill. It was something that I could empathise with. It was a lonely and humiliating experience.

After that, I went out to look for some new outfits. I was aware that purchasing a new clothing was an effort to alter the 'me' that others saw on the outside in the hopes that my inner self would also adjust.

We walked down the beach for the most of the day. As the beginning of spring approached, there were not many people around to discuss it with. After a long day of work, I decided that I deserved to spoil myself with a fancy dinner. When you are by yourself, economies of scale may be really helpful. I could really splurge on myself for the same amount of money as two dinners. I went back to my hotel after making a reservation at a beachfront restaurant for eight o'clock the next evening. The television programme I was watching was a comedy special, and I found myself laughing out loud for the first time in what seemed like months.

I showered, got dressed, and admired my appearance in the full-length mirror that was in my room. It felt like I had just turned sixteen all over again, not knowing what the night would bring for me. It was like experiencing one's own rebirth. If I were to start again, I would go into the world with my head held high. I had gone much too long wearing the same old clothing.

The meal was delicious. Chablis served with sea bass for a delicious meal. On top of it, I put down a chocolate custard topped with whipped cream. After adding two brandies, everything was let to sit and ferment in my stomach for a while.

Following my supper, I went for a stroll down the beach. In spite of the absence of light, the stars shone brightly. Their light seemed to be reflected by the plethora of little shells that were scattered over the wet sand towards the edge of the ocean. Perhaps it was the wine, but I had the strangest mental image in which I was standing on the beach and the sky was underneath me. An oasis of tranquilly in the midst of the never-ending din of contemporary life was provided by the night's pervasive feeling of stillness.

The droning sound of cars and aeroplanes constantly passing above. At that point in time, the disruptions had stopped occurring altogether.

The sound of the sea's movement as it approached to caress the shore was eerily similar to the sound of the earth resigning itself to the fact that humanity seemed to have complete control over it. I stayed still, kept an eye out, and listened for as long as it took to convince me that my place in the cosmos was equivalent to that of a shell on that beach. Surprisingly, the idea gave me a sense of security and comfort.

After walking back to the hotel, I changed into my new clothes and hung them up. I had a relaxed feeling. Even the heartburn I had before going to bed appeared to be for a good cause. Once again, I had a dreamless night of sleep.

I got out of bed at 10 o'clock. On the other hand, the mirror of the intelligent guy I had seen the night before had morphed into the image of my own father. I was not interested in having breakfast, so I made my way back to the beach after leaving the restaurant. I got lost at the water's edge and went about staring at the stars that were still embedded in the sand. I glanced at, and even sometimes picked up, a few little white stones. I have no idea why I did it, but I stuffed the stones that caught my eye into my pockets as quickly as I could.

Cliffs stood guard over the water, as if they had a solemn responsibility to do so. When the wind was blowing, the ocean might act like a naughty kid, but for the most part, it was calm and well-behaved. There were moments, however, when the ocean was encouraged to act out of control.

I was intrigued by the cliffs because they had alternating layers of distinct hues. The passage of time was being represented by the structures in a variety of ways.

They were like the several layers that might be seen in my life at the time. They were the layers that chronicled the tale of my life from the beginning of its tumultuous history to this moment of peace at the beach and to my existence on my own in my new refuge.

And life is shown via the many narratives. Although each layer is distinct, taken together they make up the whole of who I am, much as the cliff itself is composed of a series of tiers of varying heights.

I finished settling my account, took my old life to a charity shop, and then drove back to my new life, which consisted of me packing my old clothes into the bag that my new ones had been in, and wearing my old clothing.

Mantras Are Both Powerful Tools And Powerful Tools In Their Own Right.

They are an intimidating group. They date back many years. It is effective. The word 'mantra' comes from two different Sanskrit terms. The first one is manas, which might be translated as "mind," and it supplies the phrase "man." The 'three' that is represented by the second syllable comes from the Sanskrit word tra. As a result, the term mantra, when taken in its purest form, means "three sounds that programme the mind." At its most fundamental level, mantra is a technique that the mind employs in order to gradually liberate oneself from the bad energies and memories that are stored in the mind.

But getting from mantra to liberation is a magnificent experience in and of itself. The intellect broadens, deepens, and widens until it finally penetrates the core of what it is to be a part of the cosmos. The mind acquires a great deal of knowledge about the fundamental nature of the vibration of things as it travels along its path. As is common knowledge, having knowledge grants power. When it comes to mantra, this force is palpable and within reach of the practitioner.

There is a close, approximately one-to-one direct translation that may be found for mantras. When we give a small kid a stern warning not to touch a hot stove, we do our best to explain why this is the case: the youngster might be burned. However, words are not enough to adequately explain what it was like to be there. The terms 'hot' and 'burn' in relation to the 'stove' can only be defined appropriately via the experience of actually touching the stove and being burnt. In essence, there is no actual straight translation that can adequately convey what it feels like to be burnt. In a similar vein, there is no verb that can adequately describe the sensation that one feels when they accidentally poke their finger into an electrical socket. Only after we have put our hand into the socket will we have any idea what the term "shock" means in this situation. However, the term "shock" really refers to the consequence of the action of inserting one's hand into an electrical socket. In the same way, mantras are the same. The sensation that it finally generates in the one doing the defining is the one and only real definition. Many sayers have gone through the same experiences over the course of these thousands of years, and they have passed them on to the subsequent generation. A context for the experiential definition of terms has been established as a result of this tradition.

The following is an explanation of the potency of the maha mantra Om that may be found in the Upanishads:

According to the Chandogya Upanishad, "Water is the essence of Earth," which also means that "Life" is the essence of "Earth."

The essence of water is found in herbs.

Herbs have their very being in Man.

The power of language is the essence of man.

The Vedas are essentially Speech Itself.

OM is the core of all Vedic teachings.

In the scripture known as the Bhagavad Geeta, Lord Krishna is quoted as saying, "All meditation should begin with Om." In order to free up cosmic energy, the programmes offered by phenoMenon that focus on ZeNLP include creative visualisation, autosuggestion, dynamic meditation, and the chanting of mantras.

A brand-new pupil approached the Zen master and inquired about the best way to be ready for his upcoming training. The teacher elaborated, saying, "Consider me to be a bell." If you give me a light touch on the shoulder, you will hear a very faint ping. If you strike forcefully, you will hear a loud and ringing peal in response.

Simple procedure for dealing with objections

1. Pausing

2. Restate the point of contention.

3. Explain the reason for the objection

4. Take a beat

5. Respond in a straightforward and truthful manner.

The ERR approach, which can be found under the section on Presenting, is essentially the same thing as what you'll discover here.

Feelings Felt Discovered

The Feel Felt Found methodology is an effective and time-tested method for rebutting arguments that are founded on a lack of knowledge and consists of the following steps:

"I can empathise with how you are feeling. Bloggs and Company shared this sentiment, and they discovered that increasing the amount of money they spent allowed them to enjoy a far higher level of ease.

Even though it is a very ancient approach, you will see that it employs several fundamental ideas that you are familiar with from NLP. These principles include empathy, rapport, pacing states, and even Timeline.

Misleading leads

If you give it some thought, there are numerous reasons why clients ask questions other than to get an answer. Some of these reasons include the following:

To achieve the following goals: • To get a kick out of embarrassing you; • To make a good impression in front of their employer; • To answer a question that has been posed by a rival; • To buy some time; • To be able to confidently respond with "no"

I have no doubt that you can think of a great deal more justifications. The most essential thing to keep in mind is that you are wasting both your time and the time of the customer if you hurry off to discover solutions to the client's concern without first determining whether or not it is a legitimate complaint.

When you have established a good connection with a client, it is likely that both of you will feel awful about upsetting the other. When confronted with such a circumstance, the client will often devise a number of ingenious methods of declining the service, all of which have the appearance of being reasonable justifications but ultimately serve to waste time.

It is important to understand that phrases such as "I'll need to talk to my wife/husband/boss" or "I'll need to think about it" really signify "no" and should be handled as such.

Consider the implications. Let's imagine you put a lot of effort into developing a sales process, and when you deliver the product to the client and ask for the business, the client asks, "Does it come in green?"

You may feel annoyed that the client did not disclose this earlier; thus, you may decide to verify with your company's technical or marketing personnel, which results in the purchase being delayed once again. If the customer just answered "no," your options would be to either walk away or investigate what may be lacking in either the customer's perspective or your knowledge of the customer's requirements. If the customer simply replied "no," your options would be to either walk away or pursue what may be lacking in either perception. This saves time for both parties, and any course of action will be more productive than responding to a question that the client did not need you to address in the first place.

When you are in a scenario where you are competing with another business and a client asks you questions about one of the other businesses' products, this might put you in a precarious position. The salesperson who has the best connection with the client will often prepare the consumer with questions for them to ask each of the other bids. There are occasions when they are difficult to see, and they relate to aspects that the product of the competition supports but that yours does not. Because they pertain to proprietary qualities or trade marks, the inquiries are often awkward and immediately reveal information about the buyer's associations. This is because the queries are trying to gather information about the purchaser.

When it comes to responding to tenders, this is one of the most crucial things to look for, since it will tell you who was responsible for writing the tender. Do not assume that the competition is fair just because the procedure for awarding contracts seems to be objective. End users often are experts at exploiting the restrictions that the finance department places on the selection of suppliers, in addition to knowing precisely what they want and who they want to work with.

If someone asks you a question or you come across a written need that doesn't seem to be in simple English, it's a good idea to type the question or requirement into Google using quotation marks to see what results come back.

Because the clarifying stage will expose a question that has no actual need behind it, the best approach to flush out red herrings is probably to employ the basic objection handling procedure that was discussed before. This is because the process will disclose a question that has no genuine need behind it.

The Pace of the Future

You may lead the consumer through the decision point by using a conversational Timeline. This will allow the client to feel comfortable with their choice and reduce the likelihood that they would "undecide."

Although it is often believed that buyer's regret is caused by the consumer changing their mind after making a purchase, I do not think this to be the case. When faced with a difficult choice, we often go back and forth between available options, mentally putting ourselves in those situations to get a sense of how we might react. If someone pressures us for a decision, we will provide the present status of that process rather than the final state of that process. After that moment, we are unable to alter our thoughts, and the cycle process just continues as normal since it hasn't been given the time it need to finish on its own accord.

This is a warning indication that a crucial piece of information is lacking, which results in your natural decision-making process being short one step.

When you go to a restaurant that offers a buffet with unlimited food, do you ever take some time to think about what you want to eat before you place your order? You are able to have everything! Compare this to the anxiety that individuals feel when they are trying to decide what to get from a menu: "If I get the beef, then I can have red wine, but the chicken looks really good, but then I should have white wine, and I really want red wine tonight."

The following is the next step in the chain of reasoning:

White wine comes after beef, then chicken, then red wine, and finally white wine.

And you continue to go around in circles until the waiter comes over and forces you to make a choice, which you then have to sit and think about until you actually receive your meal and start eating, since at the moment at which the waiter takes your order, you still haven't made a decision. And so you continue to go around in circles until the waiter comes over and forces you to make a decision. You place your order according to whatever point in the loop you are now at, but you have not really decided anything yet.

It's important to keep in mind that individuals seldom alter their views; rather, they continue to think about and consider options for a choice they have not yet chosen. We are a reliable and consistent species. The illusion of inconsistency or indecision is that individuals are forced to explain choices that they have not yet made. The truth is that we compel people to articulate decisions that they have not yet made.

According to conventional wisdom in the field of sales, you should do all in your power to keep your consumers in the "buying mode" rather than in the "owning mode." There is a specific Swedish furniture business that appears to disagree with this, and the creator of the firm is wealthier than Bill Gates. This store is well-known for its flat pack meatballs, weirdly called kitchen contraptions, and legal attitude to other people referencing its brand name. What are your thoughts?

Following are the steps that are involved in making a decision: First comes information, then comes decision, then comes ownership.

Data or information

You are completely unaware that you need the product or that it even exists at this moment in time. In order to formulate the criteria for your selection, you will first need to collect some background information.

Make a choice

You are now in a position to use your natural decision-making process to make a choice since you have accumulated sufficient information at this point.

acquisition of

Now that you've made your choice, you're curious about how you may get your hands on the goods in question. You are interested in learning about the available payment methods, the delivery possibilities, and whether or not the item will fit through your front door, among other things.

The item is now in your possession and will become an integral part of your routine moving forward.

This shop, which we will refer to as "Aeki," walks you through the procedure in the other direction of how it is often done. What is their secret to success? In what ways does it manifest itself? In what ways might you use the same basic idea?

Some furniture stores stock their warehouses with couches and scatter tables, plants, and other accessories here and there to give the impression that the space is more lived in than it really is. Aeki are capable of creating full rooms, replete with working televisions. If you travel to Aeki, you should pause for a minute to observe the young couples who are having the vivid delusion that they are in a genuine "dream home" while sitting in these settings. They will say things like, "our wedding picture will look nice on the wall, and that clock your mother gave us will just fit perfectly on that shelf," and you will hear them say these things.

If you possess anything, you must have purchased it at some point, and if you purchased it, you must have made the decision to purchase it before you actually purchased it. Our brains are quite adept at filling in the blanks when presented with a scenario that simulates a result that will occur in the future. It's almost as if we concoct a fictitious recollection of the buyer purchasing the item, which assumes that they chose to purchase the item at some point in the past.

In times gone by, we referred to this kind of situation as the "puppy dog close." When you finally have the chance to pet the puppy, you won't want to get go of it again.

You are in possession of information that people of the past did not possess. You don't even have to physically hand the consumer a dog; all they have to do is see themselves with one.

For the time being, let's simply circle back around to the concept of "buying mode." When I was younger, salespeople used to tell me that it was important to keep consumers in the "buying mode" so that they would consider purchasing from me. I can still remember what they said. Keep them focused on signing the order form rather than allowing them to become distracted by talking about what they'll do with it and where they'll put it.

In light of the four stages of the process that have been described above, I have an alternative suggestion for you: keep your consumers in the "decision mode."

Consider the following proposition as food for thought: When you purchase something simple like a chair, you don't invest in the most expensive one available. You end up purchasing the one that you were either considering at the time you made your choice or sitting in at the moment you made it. The process of making a choice is not influenced in any way by any of the characteristics that are often referred to as "decision factors."

It's nothing more than a thought. Consider this the next time you find yourself in a decision-making situation or see someone else doing so.

The following is a selection of instances of queries to which I have lately heard answers provided by salespeople:

What We Sell Educating Yourself: a Question Where is the testing facility that is most convenient for me?

Some footwear Do you have a selection of lace colours available?

Meeting or presentation Where exactly is the location of the conference?

Now, don't they seem like fantastic opportunities to make a purchase? It does not seem so. They are taking ownership of the questions. They inform you that the prospective buyer has moved beyond the stage of choice and is now seeing themselves as the owner of the goods. Traditionally, salespeople have been taught to become enthusiastic at this stage because, if the client is expressing a query or an issue like this, it must mean that they are thinking about purchasing the product, which is a clear buying signal. Is that right? No.

This is a warning indicator that they have mentally moved on from the idea of purchasing the merchandise. Would you order a starter if you had already finished your coffee, eaten your mint, and paid the bill if you were at a restaurant? It is much too simple for a prospective customer to say "no" and walk away without making a purchase, unless the very idea of having the item in my possession arouses such a strong need that I cannot put off making the purchase any longer. Simply envisioning themselves as owners of the product is enough to satiate their demand, thus they are no longer in need of the actual commodity.

In the Aeki instance, the order of events is quite significant. It guides you to a choice, but it does so in the 'wrong' path. It is essential that you retain the client at the decision stage until they have made a commitment in order for us to go in the 'correct' way when approaching a choice.

The following are some ideas that may be considered for how the salespeople mentioned earlier might have responded to those questions:

The Consumer: Retail Associate:

Where is the testing facility that is most convenient for me? Are you implying by asking this question that you have already made up your mind to enrol?

Do you have a selection of lace colours available? I am able to inspect the actual box of the shoes that you are interested in purchasing on your behalf.

Where exactly is the location of the conference? Do you have any specific conditions that you need the venue to meet in order for you to make a decision?

Remember that these are not the "right" replies; rather, they are just different from the ones that were initially given, which were motivated more by a desire to answer the question than by a want to keep the prospect focused on deciding whether or not to make a purchase.

All I'm trying to say is that you shouldn't get too enthusiastic when a prospect asks you a question about "owning mode," since doing so diverts their imagination away from the act of making a choice. Your first emphasis should be on convincing them to go with your recommendation, and only after that should you assist them in taking ownership of the product or service. If you don't, there's a chance that they'll walk away from the experience with positive emotions towards the product, but without a compelling reason to purchase it.

Consider the situation in this light. Imagine you are in the business of selling fantasies. I'm referring to the fantasies that go through your head when you sleep. Do you want the individual to see themselves having all of the wonderful fantasies they could have before they have even purchased them? Wouldn't it be the same thing to have nice dreams if you only imagined having them? If people have already seen themselves living the ideal, then what is the point of making a purchase?

The idea that individuals purchase to fulfil requirements is one perspective on the sales process. As you'll learn today, visualising something in adequate detail is nearly as good as possessing the item itself in terms of the sensation that it creates. This is true whether you're envisioning something positive or negative. For example, if I desire a new automobile, I might try to picture myself driving a brand-new Aston Martin. While this would not be nearly as satisfying as really driving one, it would provide some relief in the short term and would be cheaper than spending £90,000. It is the responsibility of the salesperson to ensure that the only way for me to get that sensation is to actually purchase the product in question. And for him to do that, he has to keep me in the state of having to make a choice.

During A Session Of Self-Hypnosis, There Are Several Things That Should Be Avoided At All Costs

Let's take a good look at the things that we need to avoid from doing in order to guarantee that our self-hypnosis works wonderfully and gets us the best possible results. Now that we have seen all of the fantastic ideas that we can use to ensure that our self-hypnosis works wonders and gets us the best possible results, let's take a good look at those things!

Avoiding Common Mistakes in Self-Hypnosis

The following is a list of things that you need to steer clear of performing if you want your self-hypnosis session to be a resounding success.

• You shouldn't expect to get the massive effects that you're looking for right now. It's possible that some individuals may have more success than others in rapidly attaining the goals they have set for themselves via the process of self-hypnosis, but for most people, it will take at least a little bit of time. Self-hypnosis is a talent that, like to any other ability, has to be cultivated over time in order to get the optimum outcomes. This is the most crucial point to take away from this discussion.

You need to keep in mind that it is just a talent, even while it is true that everyone may make use of this expertise to accomplish their personal or professional objectives, but you also need to keep in mind that it is only a skill. If you are unable to master it right away, give it some time, and you will be pleasantly surprised by the outcomes.

You only need a little bit of patience, and you will discover that your perseverance will pay off in the end. All you need is a little bit of time. Therefore, make it a point to practise hypnosis every day and see the rapid improvement in your abilities that this will bring about.

• If you're feeling weary, avoid engaging in self-hypnosis sessions. It's possible that the first thing you want to do when you're exhausted is engage in a session of self-hypnosis in the hopes of feeling better, but doing so is not a good idea at all. When you are calm and in a good mood, you will discover that you are able to get the most out of your self-hypnosis session and get the greatest potential outcomes.

Therefore, it is a pretty smart idea to carry out this procedure right after you get out of bed in the morning once you wake up. When you reach that point, you will have the vitality necessary to take the session of self-hypnosis to an entirely new level.

- Take care not to engage in excessive practise with regard to this. When it comes to your self-hypnosis sessions, the very last thing you want is to get uninterested in them. The easiest way for this to take place is if you engage in the process of self-hypnosis much more often than is recommended.

You can be putting in too much time with your hypnotic trance practise, or you might even be doing it too often throughout the day. Both of these things might be a problem. Therefore, it is a very good idea to restrict it to not more than three times a day, and not more than around twenty minutes each session. This is something that was touched on before.

- You should avoid using a voice that you are unable to connect with in any way. If you are utilising a pre-recorded voice for your hypnotic sessions, such in the case of an MP3 that you could have downloaded, then you will discover that in order to get the greatest results, you need to be able to resonate with the voice and even the manner of delivery. This is the case even if you are using an MP3 that you have downloaded. It's possible that you find a masculine voice more appealing than a female one.

It's possible that you may like a substantial amount of background music during your hypnotic sessions. In order to get the most out of your hypnotic session, you need to figure out what works for you the best and ensure that it is compatible with your frequency.

• Don't force anything to feel different during your self-hypnosis; instead, just go with the flow of your experience. When it comes to that hypnotic trance that they have put themselves into, a lot of the time individuals do not feel the way they anticipated when it comes to the process of self-hypnosis, and this is one of the primary reasons why people give up on the process. Instead of frantically attempting to make anything happen, the idea is to go with the flow and allow it happen to you rather than trying to force it to happen.

You may notice that you get the sensation of floating or perhaps of being in a dreamy state. This is quite normal. Because everyone's experience of self-hypnosis is unique, you shouldn't automatically assume that you're doing anything wrong if you notice that other people are having a different reaction to the practise than you are.

• You shouldn't be concerned about remaining in that hypnotic state without waking up. A lot of individuals are terrified that they won't be able to snap out of the hypnotic trance that they've fallen into, which is something that can be incredibly disheartening to experience. Remember that there is absolutely no possibility that anything like that could ever take place since that is the most crucial thing to keep in mind here.

If you are preoccupied with breaking out of the hypnotic trance, you will not be able to give your whole attention to the hypnotic experience that you are having in the here and now. As was said earlier, it is a very good idea to prepare yourself for the end of your hypnotic state by setting an alarm that will alert you when it is time to emerge from the trance.

- Make use of a variety of reiteration strategies in order to convey to your unconscious mind the same idea that you are working to clarify. If you want to convince your unconscious mind that you are already skinny, it is best to do it in a number of different methods rather than relying on just one. During the same hypnotic session, for instance, you may imagine that you are already skinny, and at the same time, you might imagine that all of the fat that you now have is just dissolving away. When it comes to the process of visualisation, you will discover that you have a lot of room for creative expression; thus, you should put this talent of yours to good use.

As we have shown in this chapter, there are absolutely some things that you should not do if you want to guarantee that the process of self-hypnosis garners every bit of success that you want it to. If you do any of these things, you will not get the success that you desire from the process of self-hypnosis. Be sure to keep these in mind since the last thing you want is for those wonderful self-hypnosis methods to have less of an impact than they should have when it comes to the process of working towards achieving your objectives.

The power of self-hypnosis is far more than most people realise at first. However, in order to get the finest outcomes, it is necessary to carry out these steps in an entirely correct manner; for this reason, this chapter was written. You will discover that if you adhere to the appropriate steps and steer clear of the erroneous ones, you will have the ideal formula for successful self-hypnosis.

Mastery Of The Art Of Persuasion

Every single one of the strategies that I outline in this book has been vetted by industry professionals and has been tried out by a large number of individuals. What you are about to read will introduce you to the real world of persuasion and will open your mind to its possibilities.

What you must have in order to communicate effectively

When communicating with other people, you need to do it in a manner that is straightforward in order for them to comprehend what you are saying regardless of the level of education that they have attained. The world has progressed to such an extent that a great deal of complexity has been removed from numerous procedures that are used on a daily basis. We live in a society where people respond to one another with instant messaging, a smiley face, or an emoji sticker.

If you are going to express anything, you need to convey it in a manner that is straightforward and concise; if you can say it in one line, you do not need to write a paragraph. You need to utilise repetition, also known as the so-called illusion of truth, and the reason for this is that if something is repetitious, it will become familiar to you. Using simplicity on its own is not recommended. When we repeatedly hear the same message, we start to recognise the content of the communication. Because there is not much of a distinction between the actual truth and the illusion of it, politicians are able to effectively exploit it because of this fact.

When people hear a statement more than once, they give it a higher validity rating than if they had just heard it. Because of this, repetition has evolved into one of the most straightforward and extensively used forms of persuasion.

But there is a problem with repetition, and that problem arises when people analyse repetitious arguments and discover that they have poor foundations. When this occurs, the arguments always fail. It occurs on a daily basis in the scandals that are produced on the internet, which are born from a message or a picture in which the message is misinterpreted. These scandals are born from something that was posted on the internet.

During his run for the presidency in 2000, Al Gore falsely claimed that he was the one who invented the Internet. In reality, his role was to be the first political leader to understand the significance of the extensive network. Because of this, rather than bolstering his credibility, he became the target of derision. Some others even believe that it hampered his chances of becoming president. since of this, you need to bear in mind that reputation is really expensive and must be kept since it is possible for it to be ruined with just a few lines of text.

I would like to suggest that you do an experiment with your family or friends. First, divide everyone up into two groups of ten individuals each, and then pose a question to each of those groups.

Ask the first group this question: Should undocumented persons be allowed to get medical treatment?

Should illegal people be denied access to medical care? that was the second question posed to the group.

The choice of words that you made is going to have an effect on you in the future. These are the kinds of questions that have been addressed in the course of a variety of research, and the findings have shown that just 38% of people feel that medical treatment should be "denied," while 55% believe that medical care should not be provided. As a result, the disagreement stems from the underlying assumptions. The word "deny" refers to a person's personal or societal rights, both of which they have the potential to lose. Because the response of individuals who hear the query is determined by the context, "giving" you anything does not necessarily have an effect on the law.

It is also a mistake to assume that everyone has the same understanding of a certain term. For instance, in today's society, the phrases "I believe" and "I feel" are used rather often. Although, for some people, this distinction is only a matter of language, there are distinctions, although subtle ones.

Both of these statements, "I think the recovery of the economy is going to happen from one moment to the next" and "I feel that the recovery of the economy is going to happen from one moment to the next," convey the same message; however, research has shown that a seemingly insignificant change can have a significant impact on the ability of a message to persuade.

We construct the world not only with our ideas and sentiments, such as useful or pointless, helpful or detrimental, etc., but also with our emotions, whether they be fearful or comfortable, upsetting or reassuring.

In an activity that was connected to what was discussed in the preceding paragraph, a group of individuals were given a message that was intended to persuade them to donate blood. This message was shown to them while they were in the same environments in which they had constructed the world. Both messages conveyed the identical information, with the exception of one message's use of the word "think" and the other message's use of the word "feel." At the conclusion, each individual was questioned on their likelihood of donating blood in the next years.

People who thought about the world cognitively were more inclined to donate blood when the message was phrased in terms of "thinking." Those individuals who employed phrases that evoked feelings were more likely to be convinced when the word "feel" was used.

This shows that when you are trying to convince someone of anything, it is helpful to know if they are more concerned with their thinking or their emotions, so that you may tailor your message to fit their preferences.

Why Should You Get Training In Hypnotic Persuasion Skills?

Because of the harassment and intimidation I faced at school, I made the decision to study hypnotic and persuasive techniques. Despite the fact that I detest getting into physical altercations and am not a fighter, I trained in martial arts because I wanted to improve my self-control and my self-assurance.

Even more helpful was the development of tactics for building rapport that stopped bullies in their tracks. Yes, in contrast to the other communication skills trainers, I don't think rapport has anything to do with like the other person. Rather, I think it has everything to do with guiding individuals in the direction that you want them to go. The bullies were forced to pause and reflect as a result of your communication abilities. I was able to pick up on language patterns that might be used to discredit my tormentors and leave them feeling bad long after I had forgotten about them. accomplish you want to be able to accomplish this for yourself, and do you want the abilities to do it?

When I was a young adult just starting out in the working world, I wanted to establish myself, create my network of contacts, and make new acquaintances. I tried to give out the most positive impression of myself that I could. I wanted people to have a positive reaction to meeting me or thinking about me, as well as an eager anticipation of our next encounter together. Imagine the impact you might have on others if you had these talents.

As I began my career in the corporate sector, I realised the importance of properly communicating my ideas, talents, and experience. My clients, customers, and prospects required that I sell them not just my goods but also my business and, before that, myself. My coworkers, the individuals I oversaw, and the people I worked for all had periods when they required concentration and inspiration.

Skills in hypnotic persuasion may enable you do the following: • Covertly modify another person's opinions.

• Use your storytelling abilities to get through conscious opposition.

• Make use of linguistic patterns that provide the impression of several options.

- Make sure that your tone of voice and body language exude an air of power.

- Investigate your deep unconscious and make use of its motivating filters.

- Affix good feelings to oneself and attach negative emotions to others who you consider to be your competitors or rivals.

- Ensure that consumers continue to think about you or your goods over the course of their day, regardless of whether or not they want to.

It's feasible for all of these to happen. There are a lot of fast and easy NLP and Hypnotic Language Patterns that you can add into your vocabulary, and doing so will significantly boost the amount of success you have. In the next part, I will provide you with resources to help you improve these talents further.

What exactly are some examples of hypnotic language patterns?

Patterns of Language Used in Hypnosis

Hypnotic Language Patterns are a type of indirect hypnosis. They consist of interconnected groups of words and phrases that produce a certain sentence structure. Because of the way this statement is structured, it is possible for the subject (or subjects) to enter an indirect hypnotic trance without their conscious awareness.

Because of this, hypnotic language patterns are often referred to as "covert hypnosis."This gives it an ominous tone, as if you are attempting to trick your victim into doing something against their will and take advantage of them in some way.

It couldn't be farther from the truth if you tried! Your participants will be able to arrive at their own inferences when you use hypnotic language patterns. Imagine that you are attempting to persuade a buddy to go watch the same movie that you are interested in seeing. You have two options for swaying the opinion of your friend: 1) you may beg and plead with them, or 2) you can utilise hypnotic language patterns. In either instance, there is nothing malicious about your intention. The second alternative, on the other hand, is a strategy that is both meticulously organised and productive.

Let's find out how you can put your newfound knowledge of NLP and Hypnotic Language Patterns to work now that you've got the fundamentals down!

Establishing a Connection and Rapport

Rats are a common source of anxiety for a lot of people. Imagine walking into a room and hearing nothing but rats squeaking the whole time you're there. Your first instinct would probably be to slam the door and run away, or at the very least, to get out of there as quickly as possible. This is not so much due to the fact that rats might bring you damage as it is due to the fact that rats and humans are essentially different from one another. When we recognise that we are distinct from other creatures, we automatically start to be afraid of them. The same thing is true for us when we look inside ourselves. When we encounter someone who is very unlike to ourselves, our natural reaction is to view them with suspicion. For example, we could feel uneasy with strangers, individuals who adhere to a faith that is not our own, or people from other countries and their people simply because we find them unusual. This is not a coincidence since, in general, we want to avoid interacting with people we are not acquainted with. This is the purpose of developing a connection with someone via methods such as mirroring. By using these tactics, we are able to make ourselves seem less strange and more comparable to the next person. As a consequence, we are able to get rid of any emotions of anxiety or awareness that are brought on as a direct result of being unique.

Building rapport requires establishing a sense of confidence and trust with one another. Establishing a connection with someone might be pretty simple. The most fascinating aspect of this method, on the other hand, is that by using it, one has the ability to get along with almost anybody, since it instructs one in how to interact to others more effectively while simultaneously fostering stronger relationships. These abilities, on the other hand, have two sides to their coin since they may be put to either positive or negative use. We have faith that you, as a reader of our work, will make the decision to put these strategies to good use.

a reflection of

Mirroring is a powerful method that may be used to effectively build rapport. When conversing with another individual, mirroring involves imitating their subtle behaviours to some degree. You will have a sense of connection with one another as you reflect one another. Even if you just have a cursory familiarity with one another, you will get the impression that you have known each other for an aeon. You will, for the most part, be required to imitate the actions of another person. Consider the situation in which you look at yourself in the mirror as an illustration. When you lift your left eyebrow, the expression that is reflected in the mirror on your right eyebrow is the same. Even chimpanzees employ this approach to building relationships with one another since it is so fundamentally simple and yet so easily comprehended. The same method may be used in this situation, since there are certain things that you can mimic to establish rapport. They are as follows:

• Gestures • Posture • Breathing pattern • Volume and pace of speech • Tone of voice • Language • Gestures • Posture • Breathing pattern

Rapport is basically when your voices and bodies are in sync with one another in a certain manner. In point of fact, communication is often more about the combination of the speaker's body language and the tone of their voice than it is about the message that is being sent. If you are able to master control of your body language, you will be able to significantly alter how other people see you. However, similar to the development of any other ability, mirroring may take some time, and there are several degrees of mirroring that one may acquire.

Breathing, on the other hand, is the most crucial thing you can mimic since it is a component of your physiology that is performed automatically while also being the simplest to see. You may get an indication of the person in the mirror's breathing rhythm by observing their shoulders, particularly if the person in the mirror is a woman. The stomach and the chest are two other areas that you might examine. When attempting to mimic someone else's responses, keep in mind that you should do it in such a way that it seems nearly simple and subconscious on your part. At first, it could seem strange to you, but with little practise, you'll be able to imitate it with ease. When you've reached the point where the ability is second nature to you, you won't even be aware of the work you're putting in to maintain it since it will come so easily to you.

Even though there aren't any hard and fast rules for mirroring, you should be able to apply these approaches effectively virtually all of the time. For instance, you may aid mimic a person's senses by using statements like "that sounds good" and "that rings a bell" when you see that the individual primarily processes information via their hearing rather than through their vision. If, on the other hand, they are more visual, you may communicate with them by saying things like "I see" or "It looks good" when you talk to them.

If the sensations are audible, it is preferable to describe how something sounded rather than how it appeared. If the sensations are visual, it is better to describe how something seemed. Consider an additional example, such as an opera. You could feel the need to let someone know that the performance of a band was absolutely outstanding. There is, however, little use in describing the facial expressions of the crowd or explaining how the crowds were big to a person who is more auditory than visual. This is because such a person cannot see the crowds. It would be to their advantage, though, if you described the how the violin sounded in comparison to the piano and how the voices of the performers came through. An description of the size of the audience, how the artists seemed while they were performing, the responses on the faces of the people in the crowd, and other such details would be appreciated by a person who is primarily visual. The use of words in such a way helps to create a mirrored effect, which is what generates the attention and likeability that is associated with this method.

You may establish rapport with a person by mirroring the way they use their body language. Be aware, however, that mirroring body language is not in any way a kind of imitation, even though it may seem like it. As was said before, you should avoid imitating every action since it could seem artificial, which might disrupt rapport and prevent any further communication from taking place. You should thus let the other person to take the lead, and you should follow after them and imitate their movements, just like you would if you were dancing. Take your time while imitating, for instance, when someone leans backward, take around 20 to 30 seconds to perform the same thing so that they are not able to consciously pick upon your motions.

In addition to this, it will seem natural and not artificial. The opposite impact will occur if you begin the process too quickly. Make sure that you match facial gestures well so that it does not come across as ridicule and does not make the other person feel offended. You can do things with your face, such as smiling back at someone who grins at you, as long as you don't go overboard with it. For example, you can smile back at someone who smiles at you. Your partner's subconscious will pick up on these gestures and lead him or her to believe that the two of you are similar, which will result in emotions of intimacy between the two of you.

When trying to match voices, it is vital to have a fundamental understanding of the tempo and tone of the person. This technology is helpful and efficient, particularly in the field of sales or if you are restricted to phone calls, both of which are good reasons to use it. To achieve maximum efficiency on both ends, a method of dialogue that is measured and thoughtful ought to be repeated in the same manner on both sides. Take careful notice of the loudness and rhythm utilised to respond in order to do this task successfully. It may take some time and effort to get the cadence of a discussion just perfect, but with enough practise and experience, it will eventually become second nature. Considering all of the resources that are at our disposal, it is possible that it might be beneficial to engage in some voice matching practise.

Pacing and guiding is just another instrument at your disposal; use it effectively. You can see that we describe how to pace the person you are chatting with in the tools that are located above. This effectively indicates that they are in charge of directing the discussion. However, in order for a discussion to be successful, both parties need to work together to guide the other to the conclusion that they both want. like a result, you need to get them to start replicating your movement without even realising it, just like you have been doing with them. There are a few different ways that you may take the lead in the discussion; however, it is important to keep in mind that you should always do it in a constructive manner that will be beneficial not just for you but also for the next person. To put it simply, you need to quietly flip things around so that, in due course, they will reflect your actions. In the end, if you were making a sale, for instance, you will observe that the transaction went very well since everything went according to plan.

Take, for instance: Painter Nathaniel is an artist. Nathaniel has been working hard to further his profession since he graduated from the Pratt Institute in

Brooklyn, New York, five years ago. In order to do so, he has created a studio and acquired several instruments of the trade, including paints, canvases, easels, brushes, and lights. Nathaniel has been informed by a great number of individuals that he had an intuitive ability; yet, art reviewers have been less than kind to him, and he has not yet achieved a formal gallery showing for his work. Nathaniel had an education in art in a classroom environment, and as a result, he was instructed on how to objectively and "properly" describe the artwork that he creates. To be more specific, the commonplace components of composition, form, methods, subject matter, and medium, lines, forms, values, colours, textures, space, movement, and so on; all of these are traditional and unimaginative qualities of the work of an artist.

In spite of this, Nathaniel still has the same level of enthusiasm for his work as he had before he graduated. However, he is starting to question whether or not his abilities would be better used if they were only a pastime rather than a means of earning a living. At the very least, he wouldn't feel quite as defeated and miserable in that situation.

That is, until Nathaniel's flatmate at Pratt, Brian, educated him on neuro-linguistic programming (NLP). Nathaniel, who was first hesitant and worried that the NLP techniques could be a little out there, ultimately chose to view a training film that Brian had provided him. After all, what's the worst that might happen? After coming home from his studio for a week, Nathaniel immersed himself in the movie by viewing it for many hours each evening. The next week, Brian sent Nathaniel with another movie that was more sophisticated, and after seeing it, Nathaniel's life was forever changed.

Nathaniel's perspective on painting as an art form shifted as a result of this transition. Instead of just holding a brush to the canvas and applying paint, he learned how to feel the coldness of the brush in his hand, the slightly sticky, sour, but quasi-perfumy fragrance of the oil paint, the surface roughness of the canvas, and the rise and fall of each little divot. This allowed him to create a more three-dimensional effect in his paintings. Red made his heart beat, while yellow and blue appeared to remind him of the peaceful and tranquil feeling of a beach at sunrise. He was mesmerised by how the colours influenced his emotions; red made his heart race, while yellow and blue seemed to remind him of that. Nathaniel was painting when he suddenly became aware of an inside sensation accompanying each stroke of his brush. He then realised that this was the first time in his whole life that he was experiencing his work via his senses.

Nathaniel is looked up to as a model these days. His paintings have received widespread acclaim from the art community, and he was recently featured in the July edition of Artist magazine. His work has been shown in dozens of galleries and exhibits all around the globe. Because of these factors, he was obliged to increase the amount of workspace inside his studio. Nathaniel has come to the understanding that art does not only decorate the space; rather, it causes a response in the viewer. It may enchant and inspire, but it can also haunt and bother. When guests come to visit his studio, he talks about his artwork as if he were describing it to someone who was visually impaired. He doesn't just describe a green tree; rather, he conjures up an image in their heads of a childhood memory in which they climbed the large oak tree in the back yard of their neighbours. He describes what it was like to scrape their hands against the rough bark of the tree truck, the dizzy feeling they must have had when they dangled their feet over a branch from ten feet in the air, and the intoxicating smell of green leaves on a warm summer day.

Additionally, Nathaniel will frequently explain the atmosphere of his artwork before moving on to describe the scenario. A person's mood might be thought of as a subjective state or an emotional sensation. He does not, for example, describe the truck of the tree as having straight and black sharp edges; rather, he describes the impression of the truck as shadowy, scraggy, and overweight. Nathaniel has seen a significant shift in not just his own attitude but also the attitudes of the majority of others who watch (and love) his artwork. As a result, he now enjoys sharing his newly discovered enthusiasm for NLP, and others seek to him for direction and instruction.

The conduct of

Behaviour is the second element of the model for the formation of habits. The reaction that is shown in response to a stimulus is known as behaviour. It is intended to serve two primary reasons, the first of which is to receive something that an individual wants, and the second of which is to avoid acquiring something that they do not desire. It is essential to keep in mind that practically all behaviours are picked up from the significant persons in our lives. Although some of it is the result of reactions, all of it can be seen and measured.

This indicates that not only is a person's behaviour apparent to other people, but it is also a mirror of the person's mental state. For instance, if a person is upset, it will show in their behaviour, which may manifest as a changing face expression or an angry bodily response. This behaviour varies from person to person and is not consistent; rather, it is dependent on the individual's learnt behaviour, which is gleaned by studying the behaviour of others while engaging in previous experiences.

As I've already said, behaviour may also be measured. This indicates that it is conceivable for a third party to characterise the behaviour after it has been seen by them. For instance, one person may see another person get upset and then relate how they themselves reacted to seeing it. This behaviour may be changed in order to reveal a consequence that is desired.

The Repercussions

The last part of the equation is the consequence, which arises as a direct result of the behaviour phase. One way to think about it is as the response of one's surroundings to a certainbehaviour. The behaviour will, as a direct outcome of the action, have some kind of consequence. For instance, if a person responds to a certain circumstance in a bad way, then the outcome is almost certainly going to be unpleasant as well. If someone were to get angry and smash a vase into the floor, it is only natural that the vase would shatter, and the angry person would be responsible for cleaning up the mess. In the same way that behaviour may be measured, so can its consequences.

If you are completely familiar with the procedure that I outlined above, you have the ability to modify it so that it works better for you. It requires having an understanding of the signals, adhering to a routine, and making use of the reward or consequence. The trick here is to strive for the desired outcomes while altering both the antecedent and the incentives; if you do this, the behaviour will adapt on its own in accordance with the new circumstances.

If you are attempting to acquire a new skill, but you find that purchasing books in order to reach this goal does not motivate you enough to study the content, then switching over to taking courses online may urge you to study the topic to a greater extent.

In a similar vein, you may alter the reward in order to bring about the desired change in behaviour. For instance, if you are studying hard for an important test, you can tell yourself that if you do well, you will finally get to purchase that cool new toy or outfit you've had your eye on for ages. Both of these things have the potential to serve as a driving force for you to adjust the behaviour enough.

The strategy described above is quite effective, in my experience, for modifying more broad patterns of behaviour. However, the patterns of thought that people engage in rather than merely their behaviours are the primary focus of our attention in this context. Despite the fact that the two aspects are somewhat intertwined. This is the goal that genuine NLP works towards achieving. To do this, you will need to adopt a new strategy and look at things from a somewhat different perspective.

Several Factors That Should Be Kept In Mind

We have offered a very easy-to-follow description of how to make your own anchor in the step-by-step method that has been provided above; nevertheless, there are a few extra things that you should keep in mind as you think about them before and throughout the development of your anchor.

The purpose of an anchor is not limited to boosting confidence. You have the ability to build an anchor that focuses on and facilitates the recollection of a wide range of experiences or emotions that you have encountered in the past. You will be able to anchor it in your mind if you can recall it.

You are free to choose whatever portion of your body to use as an anchor. You may use any portion of your body that you are able to physically reach, such as your finger, wrist, arm, leg, or toe, as an anchor place. Always keep in mind that in order to recall a specific event, sensation, or emotion, you will need to be able to physically touch the spot that serves as your anchor. Therefore, you want the position of your anchor to be as accessible as possible. In point of fact, a lot of individuals utilise the lobe of their ear as an anchor position. Pulling on your ear while being interviewed could appear a little strange, but if you can do it in a way that is not obvious, go ahead and do it. Do whatever seems to bring you the most success.

Keep in mind that it is necessary to re-establish your anchors on a regular basis. Our memories and the things that attach us might become less vivid with time. Every once in a while, you should make an effort to reexperience the feelings or experiences that are most important to you.

They Don't Care About the Consequences Even If They Get Caught Because It's None Of Their Business.

Psychopaths, in general, are often unable to feel fear or regret, and as a result, they are typically unfazed when they are caught in the act of committing a crime. The excitement that they would have felt if they had been successful in accomplishing whatever it was that they had set out to do is incomparably greater than the pain that they are going to have to endure as a result of the punishment that is going to be inflicted on them. They respond to being caught in the same way that experienced businessmen do when a business risk doesn't pay off: not with regret, but possibly with a sense of eagerness and giving an uncanny vibe of wanting to do a better job the next time the opportunity presents itself. A penalty that is just temporary, and nearly nothing for them. Because it won't continue forever, it just gives the psychopath time for reflection and re-strategizing, so that when he is released from his sentence, he will be better prepared for more covert tactics for carrying out his psychopathic acts.

Psychopaths are the most pathological liars there are.

Psychopaths are so skilled at deception that they often polish the art of lying to the point that their fabrications are easily believed. They come at you with such a straight face, and they also conjure up extremely credible stories. They are incredibly convincing. Their capacity to live so well is inextricably linked to the fact that they are so vehemently committed to their plan that reality doesn't seem to be any different from what they have envisioned for themselves. In addition to this, they are able to quickly create credible narratives revolving around their schemes, which in turn helps them attract customers. Additionally, they are quite good at keeping a chronological record of their lives. This gives them the ability to tell more connected falsehoods in the event that they are confronted with the truth about the lies they have been telling. The lies that a psychopath tells are so well crafted that, in the event that those lies are exposed, the victim is left in disbelief at how naive they were to have believed the lie in the first place.

Psychopaths often have a history of violent behaviour against their siblings when they were still children.

Because psychopathy is a feature that manifests itself very early in life, those who have it are always more likely to have a history of violence against others from childhood. This is because psychopaths are unable to feel any kind of love, not even for their own siblings, which makes it difficult for them to form healthy relationships with others. They are also likely to have a history of mistreating animals for no reason other than the sheer enjoyment of it. Psychopaths who were disturbed as children are often seen as relishing the opportunity to get into trouble for the sake of the entertainment it affords them. The Problem Child is an example of a film that replicates, maybe in a comedic way, what it could be like to have childhood psychopathy. Another possibility is the movie "Home Alone." In point of fact, though, it is not quite as gorgeous as it seems to be on television.

Modulations of the Voice

A person's learning type may also be discerned rather accurately by listening to their speech patterns. Interact with other people and pay close attention to the language that they use. Be on the lookout for hints that suggest the learning type of the other person. Certain words, such as "I see your point," are indicative of a person who learns visually. These are telltale characteristics of an auditory learner: "This sounds familiar." If you say anything like "I think I got it," you are probably a kinesthetic learner. These patterns of speech are also helpful for determining the sort of learning style that other people have so that you may adapt to their language and communicate with them in a simpler and more efficient manner.

terms such as "look," "see," "reveal," and "clear" are often used by those who learn mainly through their visual sense; those who learn primarily through their auditory sense use terms such as "listen," "harmonise," "tell," and "squeak;" and those who learn primarily through their kinesthetic sense will use words such as "solid," "grasp," "catch on," and "tap into;" etc. When it comes to acquiring knowledge and having an awareness of the world, each of us has a main sense that we favour, despite the fact that our senses often overlap (Masters, 1991).

The importance of effectively communicating knowledge will become clear to you after you have a better grasp of how the human mind operates. It is up to the manner in which information is presented to determine whether or not a person will be open to it.

Cues for the Eye's Access

When a person is talking, you may tell what kind of thoughts they are having by observing their eye movements to see whether they are thinking in terms of images, sensations, or sounds. This supplies you with information about the individual's preferred mode of academic achievement.

In most cases, the eyes will migrate to the left or right depending on which side of the face is the subject's dominant side. For instance, if the person is right handed and he is thinking back on a memory, he will glance to the left; but, if he is thinking of something new or if he is lying, he will look to the right. This is because the brain processes information from left to right. If a person is recalling something they have heard or creating something new, they will look laterally or to the side. If a person is recalling how something felt or imagining how it would feel, they will look downward (Bandler, 1975).

Practising your accent by listening to the way others talk to each other at a coffee shop or on television is one technique to improve your speaking ability. Also, bear in mind that this is not always 100% accurate; so, if a guy is right handed and he's looking up and to the right, don't necessarily assume that he's lying to you about anything just because he's looking in that direction.

Creating an atmosphere conducive to learning

The environment in which the activity takes place influences the degree to which a person is receptive to the information being presented. According to the findings of study, in order for participants to enter into the mindset of learning, facilitators need to subtly indicate the learning style of the participants.

Setting up posters and visuals that provide the trainees with a fast preview of the topics that are going to be discussed is an effective technique to accomplish this goal while conducting training sessions for newly hired staff. A favourable reaction from the respondents is also induced when light and colour are added to the environment. In order for the mind to be able to receive information in a timely manner, it has to be stimulated.

During boardroom meetings, you may improve everyone's disposition by clearing the space of any clutter or extraneous things that divert attention away from the subject at hand. The architects came to the conclusion that even the physical environment of a boardroom might influence creative output. They advocate having a room that is bright and has enough of space because it creates an environment that is conducive to learning and gives the mind more flexibility. A confined and crowded location, on the other hand, might put one's thoughts in a box and give one the impression of being hemmed in, which can make the participants feel uneasy.

How Can I Reprogram My Mind To Get Rid Of Stress, Anxiety, Fear, And Depression? What Are The Steps?

The mind is an extremely intricate component of the brain. It is able to adapt to new circumstances when they are brought to its attention by a human. As a result, it is possible for individuals to retrain their brains in order to triumph over negative mental states such as anxiety, fear, and sadness. There are standard procedures that may assist someone in reprogramming their thinking. In order for these steps to be effective, one must have a strong desire for the kind of life they want to leave behind, put in the effort to select what those rules will be, and commit to following those principles.

When one is getting their mind ready for anything, they have to determine what it is they want to get out of the process. This is the capacity of an individual to get clarity on the result that is wanted. Clarity has its own power because it enables a person to remain motivated throughout the process by providing them with a more clear vision of the conclusion they seek. It provides the brain with the instrument it needs to transform a vision into a reality.

Another component that will play a critical role throughout these processes is commitment. This characteristic helps the subconscious mind rid itself of self-doubt, which is beneficial. A person may rid themselves of negative ideas and serve as a driving force towards their own accomplishment when they commit to something. This is the actual power that comes from rewiring a person's mentality at a subconscious level. It is necessary for the individual to find resolution inside themselves before the mind may be reprogrammed. A person is required to provide their complete commitment and to keep a record of the circumstances. After then, she or he is able to exert complete control over the mind by going through a series of processes leading to mental stability and making mental adjustments.

During the mental processes described above, the following are the stages that are employed to retrain the mind:

Taking some time off for ourselves

When a person is dealing with any of these mental states, it is quite challenging for that individual to think coherently. Because of worry, despair, tension, and dread, a person's mind might get overwhelmed and overrun by unstableness, and this is the reason why. It is strongly recommended that a person take some time to physically relax as the first and most vital step in any situation. A period of time ranging from fifteen to thirty minutes is enough time for a person to engage in a distinct activity. Activities that put the body in motion, like walking, bathing, or cooking, might help the body feel more at ease. The mind is able to reestablish its equilibrium and rid itself of various mental states as a result of this.

Through all of these mental states, breathe.

When a person is experiencing a mental condition such as anxiety, sadness, stress, or fear, it is recommended that they avoid fighting the circumstance even if they start to experience physical symptoms such as increased heart palpitations or perspiration. If it is impossible for a person to move about, they are expected to locate a tranquil area or remain in the position they are in. The next step that is instructed to a person is to lay their hand on their tummy and make an effort to breathe gently and deeply. This procedure is working towards an essential objective for the mind. It allows the mind to relax, adapt to the circumstances, and ultimately prevail despite them.

Confront the mental condition that you were in at the moment.

Anxiety, despair, stress, and terror are the four states of mind that the mind is thought to be able to triumph over. No matter which one a person is up against, they are expected to confront it head-on regardless of which one it is. Ignoring the mental condition may make it impossible for the mind to cope with the situation at hand, making it intolerable. However, when confronted with it on a regular basis, the brain is able to conquer it since it has become used to the challenge. As a result, doing an activity repeatedly may assist in the reprogramming of the mind, which is necessary in order to triumph over negative mental states.

The thoughts of those who are the worst.

It is recommended that a person attempt their best to picture the worst possible outcome that might occur. It is very recommended that from this point on, he or she keep in mind that he or she is in complete command of the circumstance. The mind is better able to prepare for how to avoid potentially destructive situations when it is aware of what the worst-case scenario may be. The mind is adaptable and may make adjustments so that it corresponds to the most likely outcome of the mental state. Although not all situations are the same, a person should never allow his or her mind to reason right up to the edge of the acceptable range. This assists in reprogramming the mind to have a new perspective on the issue at hand and in reprogramming the mind itself.

Examine the evidence that has been provided.

The data that has been presented is helpful in retraining the mind. When experiencing negative mental states such as anxiety, despair, stress, or terror, individuals are advised to reflect on their own personal experiences or the experiences of others from their past. There are several success stories of persons in these mental states when given to them, as well as a prior success if a person was presented by a situation that was comparable to the one being discussed here. When confronted with such circumstances, the mind is able to become more at ease and positive as a result of this. When the mind is calmed down, it is able to function at its highest potential, which may assist in the reprogramming of the mind and the conquering of certain mental states.

Don't stress out about being flawless.

These mental conditions, which include anxiety, sadness, tension, and fear, are periodically encountered in the life of a typical individual. Because of this, it is unhelpful for a person to have the mindset that their life would always turn out to be flawless and free of defects. It's not uncommon to have a bad day, but the silver lining is that you can power through it. A person is expected to be aware, while simultaneously in these mental states, that there are no related creating methods for getting over. It's because various people have used unique ways of thinking to extricate themselves from comparable mental conditions that have been offered to them. This assists in preparing the mind to think beyond the norm of society in order to discover answers, which in turn creates a reprogramming of the mind and an overpowering of the mental moods.

Imagine yourself in a peaceful setting.

When a person experiences negative mental states such as worry, despair, tension, or fear, it is recommended that they think about a joyful location instead of dwelling on these negative emotions. A person is instructed to shut their eyes and make an effort to clear their mind by visualising a location that is peaceful, secure, and tranquil. One is able to conjure up images of strolling or unwinding on a breathtaking beach, sitting in his or her home watching one's preferred television programme, or recalling a cherished memory from their younger years. This helps to quiet the mind and body, making it easier for the body to reprogram itself to tranquilly via fictitious idea or memories. As a result, it is easier to overcome the mental condition since it calms the mind.

Discuss it in detail.

The brain of a person may benefit tremendously by discussing difficult emotions and states of mind, such as worry, despair, tension, or terror. When a person confides in others about the specific mental condition they are experiencing, their mind is able to get solace from such conversations. These individuals may be close relatives, close friends, or even work colleagues. The mind is capable of gaining fresh comprehension in order to triumph over the mental condition. This, in turn, leads to the retraining of the mind, which ultimately results in the complete and utter conquest of the existing mental state.

Take the time to master the fundamentals.

A significant number of individuals in today's society turn to harmful behaviours as a means of overcoming negative emotions such as worry, despair, tension, or fear. The use of alcoholic beverages or illicit substances is one of these behaviours that should be avoided. There are perfect practises that are advocated that assist the brain take it easy, reprogram, and conquer the mental condition. These practises may be found here. These ideal practises, which are also fundamental, include getting a decent night's sleep, eating a balanced meal, and exercising.

Gain for the individual

This is the last phase in the process that will assist reprogramme a person's mind and make it successful in responding to different mental states that it is exposed to. The human mind is very complex in terms of the ways in which it operates. When it is rewarded for its achievement, it serves as motivation for greater success. As a result, it is recommended that a person reward themselves if they are successful in overcoming negative mental states such as anxiety, despair, tension, or fear. A person may choose to treat themselves to a massage, an enjoyable stroll, a supper out, or any other kind of little present that will make them feel happier.

www.ingramcontent.com/pod-product-compliance
Lightning Source LLC
Chambersburg PA
CBHW050419120526
44590CB00015B/2027